I0476920

BUSINESS AND LEGAL TERMS
Copyright ©2015 by Daniel U. Acedo
Cover art and design By Daniel U. Acedo
ISBN-13: 978-1515140375
ISBN-10: 1515140377

* Read Disclaimer.

Disclaimer:

This work was created with good intentions of providing accurate information regarding the subject matter contain herein. However the author and Publisher are not engaged (or) are engaging in rendering accounting, legal, investment, or tax advice or services through this publication. If legal or other expert services are required, the services of a competent licensed professional should be sought in your state. In addition, the information in this book is up-to-date only up to the date of publication the publisher and the author of this book have no liability to any person or other legal entity in regard to any loss or damage caused either directly or indirectly by the information or use of such information contain in this book. There is no guarantee of success and caution such be used in dealing with securities, it is requested that a licensed competent attorney conducts all your affairs on your behave. All Contextual-link are property of their respective owners, they own such rights to their content and they are being reference, the author and the publisher are not claiming any right in such links.

LETTER A

Abstract- A concise summary of no more than 150 words on the face of a patent application defining the design, function, nature, structure and novelty of the claims of the patent.

AIA- An Acronym used in reference to the Leahy-Smith America Invent Act that changed the United States patent system from a "first to invent" to "first to file" that went into effect March 16, 2012 in the United States.

Arbitrary Clause- A clause in a contract in which the parties agree to solve their issues outside of court.

Acquiescence- Action or inaction which binds a person legally even though it was not intended as such.

Acceptance- In reference to contracts, an entity that assents to the terms of an offer.

Assumption of loan- Is when an entity i.e., a person assumes the loan of another via a written document. The person assuming the loan is personally liable for the loan under the doctrine of equitable subrogation See e.g. Braun vs. Creis.,183 Cal.712(1920).

Arbitrage- The nearly simultaneous purchase and sale of securities of foreign exchange in different markets in order to profit from price discrepancies. A form of hedge investment to capture slight differences in the prices of two related securities e.g., buying gold in London and selling it at a higher price in New York.

London	New York	Chg%
$5.00	$6.00	1.00+

Adverse Possession- A method of acquiring title to real property by possession for a statutory period under certain conditions, esp. a non-permissive use of the land with a claim of right when the use is continuous , exclusive, hostile, open and notorious.

Affidavit of title-(Affidavit of ownership): A written statement made under oath by the seller or grantor and acknowledge before a notary public in which the grantor (1) Identifies himself or herself and indicates marital status such as single, widow, widower, or married. (2) Certifies that since his examination of the title on the date of the contract there are no judgments, bankruptcies, or divorces against him or her, no unrecorded deeds or contracts, no repair or improvements that have not been paid for an no know defects in the title; and (3) certifies that the grantor is in possession of the premises.

Annuity- An insurance type contract in which you exchange a lump sum of money for future payments whether monthly or annually.

Account Receivable- is money to be received for goods supplied to a customer usually due within 30 days.

Account Payable- The accounts payable entry is found on a balance sheet under the heading current liabilities. Account payable is a short-term debt owed usually in 15, 30, or 60 days.

Bear Market- This term is used in the stock market and it refers to stock prices plummeting.

Bull Market- This term is used in the stock market and it refers to stock prices rising.

Business 'Good Will'- The value of a business based on location, dependability, quality or skill which affects the retention of patronage.

Bonus Value- The difference between actual rent and market rent which is based on the lease e.g., actual rent is $20,000 but the tenant is paying $10,000 under his or her lease. The lease runs for four years the bonus value is $40,000

$20,000-$10,000= $10,000x4= $40,000

Business Method Patent (Cyber Patent)- A U.S. Patent that clearly describes and claims a series of steps that as a whole constitute a method of doing business.

Breach of duty- The violation of a legal or moral duty; the failure to act as the law obligates one to act. See Negligence.

Breach of Covenant- The violation of an express or implied promise, usu. In a contract, either to do or not to do an act. See. Covenant

Breach of trust- a trustee's violation of either the trust's terms or the trustee's general fiduciary obligations; the violation of a duty that equity imposes on a trustee, whether the violation was willful, fraudulent, negligent, or inadvertent. A breach of trust subjects the trustee to removal and creates personal liability.

Breach of warranty- A breach of an express or implied warranty relating to the title, quality, content, or condition of goods sold. UCC § 2-312.

Bankruptcy- Provides for the reduction or elimination of certain debt and can provide a timeline for repayment of non dischargeable debt overtime. It also permits individuals and organizations to repay secure debts. Typically debts with real estate and vehicles pledge as collateral—often on more favorable terms to the borrower. However Independent Retirement Accounts, Home Equity and motor vehicles are protected from creditors. See Title 11U.S.C. § 552.

•Chapter 7 Bankruptcy: Allows cancellation of unsecure debts, such as credit cards and personal loans (available to individuals with primary business debts and corporations) must meet income requirements.

•Chapter 11 Bankruptcy: Allows a business to be liquidated to satisfy the business debts. Further Chapter 11 bankruptcy allow debtor to reorganize debt i.e., by repaying some debt, cancelling other debt and reconstructing the remainder debt (expensive to file.)

•Chapter 12 bankruptcy: Allows farmer debtors with annual income to adjust their debt.

•Chapter 13 bankruptcy: Allows individual debtors to preserve existing assets subject to a court approved plan under which they pay creditors of their future income.

Blanket mortgage- A mortgage secured by multiple properties or lots. A blanket mortgage is often used to secure financing for proposed subdivisions or construction of condominiums. A blanket mortgage should have a "prelease clause" integrated in the mortgage documents so that the developer taking care of the subdivision and/or the construction can obtain a release from the blanket mortgage for each lot as it is sold according to a specific schedule e.g. if a developer obtains a $500,000 blanket mortgage to cover the development of 50 lots, he might be required to pay $10,000 of principal to get each lot release from under the blanket mortgage. Land developers will usually have "special recognition" clause put in the mortgage blanket where the lender agrees to recognize the rights of each individual parcel owner, even if the developer defaults and there is a foreclosure. A blanket mortgage can also be used to purchase a home plus an adjacent vacant lot.

Bootstrapping-A method of starting a business with little or o capital.

Balance sheet- A financial statement that show the assets, liabilities and net worth of a company.

LETTER C

Crowd funding- Currently crowd funding is illegal until the "SEC" issues rules regarding crowd funding. However non-profit crowd-funding is perfectly legal. Once the SEC determines the rules regarding crowd funding under the Jump Start Our Businesses Act of 2010 then small companies will be able to raise money using an intermediary such as a "funding portal" or "Broker" register with the National Security Association.

Copyright- The right to reproduce and publicize (sell or distribute) an artistic work like a song, book or movie.

COPPA- Acronym for Children protection Act which requires operator of websites directed at children under the age of 13 to get parental permission before collecting or sharing information that could be used to identify or contact a child.

Condemnation Clause- A clause that is placed in a lease agreement which specifies goodwill and bonus value.

Choice of law-A clause in a contract in which the parties agree to follow the laws of the state in which the contract was created.

Charge card-A card like a credit card that requires to pay the full outstanding balance at the end of the billing cycle.

Credit card- A card that requires payment of only a portion with the balance subject to interest.

Contractual Covenants- One having accepted a deed to real property covered by a purchase agreement, a buyer may not generally rely on covenants of title contained in the agreement unless they're also contained in the deed.

Covenant of title- is a covenant that binds the grantor (seller) to insure the completeness security and continuance of title transferred. Covenant of title includes the covenant of seisin, against encumbrances for the right to convey, for quiet enjoyment, and warranty.

Capitation payment- is payment to a doctor to care for all healthcare plan clients.

Codicil- A supplement or addition to a will, not necessarily disposing of the entire estate but modifying, explaining, or otherwise qualifying the will in someway. In probate proceeding the codicil becomes part of the will.

Covenant- A formal agreement or promise usually in a contract.

Covenant of warranty- A covenant by which a grantor (seller) agrees to defend the grantee (buyer) against any lawful or reasonable claims of superior title by a third party and indemnify the grantee (buyer)for any loss sustained by the claim. This covenant is sometimes treated as being synonymous with covenant for quiet enjoyment.

Covenant for possession- A covenant giving a grantee or lessee possession of land.

Covenant of quiet enjoyment- A covenant insuring against the consequences of a defective title. 2. A covenant ensuring that the tenant will not be evicted or disturbed by the grantor or a person having a lien or superior title against the property. This covenant is sometimes treated as being synonymous with covenant of warranty- Also termed covenant of quiet enjoyment.

Casualty Insurance- An insurance policy that covers negligent acts and omissions that cause bodily injury, and/or property damage to third parties.

Capital stock- Amount of assets i.e. money or property contribute by stockholders to be used as the financial foundation for the corporation. It includes all classes of common and proffered stock.

Capital Resources- Any good that is used in the production of other goods. Factories, many buildings, equipment, and the like are capital resources.

Capital Structure- A corporation's financial framework, including long-term debt, preferred stock, and net worth, capital structure includes only long-term debt and equity.

Constructive Adverse Possession- Adverse possession in which the claim arises from the claimant's payment of taxes under color of right rather than by actual possession of the land.

Covenant of non claim- A covenant barring a grantor's (sellers) heir from claiming title in conveyed land.

Covenant to convey- A covenant in which the conveyor agrees to convey an estate's title to the covenantee.

Covenant to stand seised- A covenant to convey land to a relative.

Covenant of seisin- A covenant, usually appearing in a warranty deed, stating that the grantor (seller) has an estate, or the right to convey an estate, of the quality and size that the grantor (seller) purports to convey. For the covenant to be valid , the grantor (Seller) must have both title and possession at the time of the grant.

Civil Wrong- A violation of noncriminal law, such as a tort, a breach of contract or trust, a breach of statutory duty, or a defect in performing a public duty; the breach of a legal duty treated as the subject matter of a civil proceeding.

Cuspip- Committee on uniform security procedures Cuspip is owned by the American Bankers Association and is operated by the S&P Capital IQ.

Contingency-is a fee for services provided where the fee is payable only if there is a favourable result

Consignment- An agreement to pay a supplier after the goods are sold.

CIK- Abbreviation for "Central Index Key" which is used to identify the filling of a company, person, or entity in several online databases including the SEC's EDGAR online database

Clayton Act- A United States Federal statute that amended the Sherman Act that prohibits price discrimination, tying arrangements, and exclusive-dealing contracts, as well as mergers and interlocking directorates, if their effect might sustainably lessen competition or create a monopoly in any line of commerce.

Code of federal regulations- The annual collection of executive agency regulations published in the daily Federal Register, combined with previous issued regulations that are still in effect. The code of regulations is usually abbreviated as "CFR".

Collateral-Contract Doctrine- The principle that in a dispute concerning a written contract, proof of a second (but oral) agreement will not be excluded under the parol-evidence rule if oral agreements are independent of and consistent with the written contract, and if the information in the oral agreement would not ordinarily be expected to be included in the written contract.

Cognitive test- Criminal law. A test in which a criminal defendant is tested on the ability to know certain things, especially the nature of his conduct and whether the conduct was right or wrong. This test is used to determine if the defendant being accused qualifies for an insanity defense.

Convertible debt- A form of financing in which a debt obligation can be turned into equity (Stock ownership) generally upon occurrence of future financing.

Corporate Securities Law of 1968- The California statute regulating securities law in California.

California Limited Offering Exemption (See Cal.Corp.Code §25102)- See link below for Limited Offering Packet:

http://www.dbo.ca.gov/forms/doc/DBO-25102f_Instructions_Only.pdf

See California Corporation Code 25102 click the link below:
http://leginfo.legislature.ca.gov/faces/codes_displaySection.xhtml?lawCode=CORP&sectionNum=25102

California Family Rights Act-It provides leave for adoption, birth, and foster care placement

 See this link for more information:

http://www.documents.dgs.ca.gov/ohr/supervisor/DGSFMLAPolicyProcedures.pdf

Close-Corporation- A Corporation that usually has less than 35 shareholders and is less formal than an actual corporation. However all shareholder must agree to run the corporation as a close corporation and the down fall of a close corporation is the fact that the close corporation can't offer securities. Further a Close corporations is governed by both bylaws and shareholders agreements.

LETTER D

Debt-to-income ratio- A ratio used to show proportions between your debt and income and use as a percentage to show solvency.

*The new guidelines for mortgage require a debt-to-income ratio of 43% or less. See. http://files.consumerfinance.gov/f/201310_cfpb_qm-guide-for-lenders.pdf

D-U-N-S Number- A number that is required for your business to work with federal and state procurement and to establish credit. See duns & Brand Street Website to learn the basics of building credit for your business. *https://iupdate.dnb.com/iUpdate/businessCreditBasics.htm

*Also check this website to get your D-U-N-S Number:

http://www.dnb.com/get-a-duns-number.html

Due-on-sale clause- A clause in the mortgage which makes the mortgage balance due upon the assumption of the mortgage by a third party or accelerates the loan in the event of a sale or other specific transfer without the lender assenting.

Deloittes Technology 500- An index ranking the fastest growing technology, media, telecommunications, life science and technology companies in North America. Fast growing companies grow because of their constant innovation.

* Here is the link to the index: http://www2.deloitte.com/us/en/industries/technology-media-and-telecommunications/north-america-technology-fast-500.html

Declarative knowledge-(cognitive psychology): is a persons 'encyclopedia' knowledge base.

Defeasance Clause- A clause used in lease or mortgage that cancels such lease or mortgage upon certain conditions.

Debt-In reference to corporate capitalization is money borrowed by the corporation in return for promissory noted or other debt instruments. Debt capital in corporate capitalization is better than equity capitalization because it provides tax advantage both to the corporation and to the note holder. For the note holder the interest payments are taxed at regular income tax rates, but the repayment of principal is simply a return of capital, which gives rise to no individual tax income. The Corporation then its allowed to deduct the interest payments as a business expense on its tax return. Always watch your debt-to-equity ratio because banks are unlikely to lend you money if the ratio is too much debt/not enough equity.

*Word of caution: While debt capitalization is advisable be cautious with shareholder loan arrangements. Because If disproportionate amount of money is "loaned" to a "closely held corporation" rather than paid in stock, and the repayment of such loan is unduly permissive or generous the I.R.S or a court of law may find that contributions to be in essence an equity transaction contrived as debt to obtain favorable tax treatment. Therefore the tax advantage may be voided and both you and the corporation may be forced to pay regular taxes. In other words the interest payments on the loan would be considered also the return of capital would be treated as dividends as well and the corporation would not be able to deduct the interest as an expense.

LETTER E

Exchange Act- Requires that publicly traded companies make quarterly and annual reports on their financial status and business performance.

Note: All info you provide to the prospective investor must be: "accurate and not misleading in its content or omissions."

Equitable title- The interest only held by one who has agreed to purchase but has not yet closed the transaction. Such as entering into a real estate contract to purchase real but the transaction hasn't been closed due to the closing date being on a set specific date, also a person who has a right to obtain full ownership of a property or property interest.

Encumbrance- is a right to, interest in, or legal liability on real estate that does not prohibit passing title to the property but that diminishes the fair market value.

Easement- Is an interest in land owned by another entity, consisting in the right to use or control the land, or, an area above or below it, for a specific limited purpose (Such as to cross it for access to a public road.) Unlike a lease or license, an easement may last forever, but it does not give the holder the right to possess, taken from, improve, or sell the land.

Earn out Agreement- An agreement for the sale of a business whereby the buyer first pays an agreed amount up front, leaving the final purchase price to be determined by the business future profits usually the seller helps manage the business for a period of after the sale- Sometime shorten "earn-out"

Escheat- Revision of property (esp. real property) to the state upon the death of an owner who has neither a will nor any legal heirs.

Emeritus- Is a title given to a retired professional, bishop, pope, President, Prime minister or other professional.

Escape Clause- Is a contractual provision that allows a party to avoid performance under specific conditions.

Equity Capital- is a term in reference to corporate capitalization in which money or dollar value of property is transferred to a corporate entity in exchange for share of stock. An equity contribution may result in taxable income to the shareholders'

Eraser Law- A California Law that will be going into effect in 2015 allowing teenagers under 17 to erase their posting off the internet and information of the internet and that prohibits the sale of apps from marketing products and services to be considered to be for adults like tanning beds and or dietary supplements.

Equitable Subrogation- is a doctrine whereby one party who pays off the mortgage obligation of another is treated as the beneficial owner of that original obligation.

Equal Credit Opportunity Act- Makes it unlawful for any creditor to discriminate against applicant with respect to a credit transaction, on the basis of race, color, religion, national origin, sex, marital status, or age or due to the fact that the applicants income derives from public assistant programs.

Estate- All of the things a person owns: the things left by someone who has died: a large piece of land with a large house on it.

LETTER F

Form D-A U.S. Security Exchange Commission form used in regulation D Securities exemptions.

*The form can be obtain online at:https://www.sec.gov/about/forms/formd.pdf

Freedom of information Act- An act enacted by congress which allows the general public to inquire into government affair free form retaliation. The Freedom of Information Act is codified in Title 5 U.S.C. § 552 (a)

Factoring- is a method to sell your invoices to a third party in exchange they will get pay a commission for providing the capital for you to operate. For example:

There is two type of factoring:

Nonrecourse Factoring: is when a company sells its invoices to a factor, and has no liability with any uncollected invoices the factor doesn't collect.

Recourse Factoring: is when a company sells its invoices to a factor, with the promise that the company will buy back any uncollected invoices.

Franchise- Is a method of expanding your business by selling licensing the rights to use the trademarks and systems in exchange for initial franchise fees and royalties. There is three components to a franchise (1) Brand (2) Operating System (3) Ongoing support from franchisors

Franchise Investment Law- In 1970 California adopted its franchise investment law. Soon thereafter in 1979 the FTC adopted the "rule 436" to protect consumers require franchisors to disclose all material information to the prospect franchisee. See link for more information: http://www.dbo.ca.gov/Licensees/franchise_investment_law/ Here is the Califonia Corporation Code that regulates franchises in California: http://www.leginfo.ca.gov/cgi-bin/displaycode?section=corp&group=30001-31000&file=31000-31019

Federal Trade Commission Rule 436- Is a rule governing franchise offerings in the United States See link below: https://www.ftc.gov/enforcement/rules/rulemaking-regulatory-reform-proceedings/franchise-rule

FHA Title II 203K Loans- This is a type of loan that is insured by the federal government i.e. The United States Federal Housing Administration insures the lender against lost. The 203k loan is used to buy properties that need repairs' to be done. The 203k loan is also used to buy property that is "inhabitable" and can't qualify for a conventional mortgage. Here is how a FHA 203k loan works:

Let's say you want to buy a home that needs windows and a kitchen. An FHA 203k lender would then give you the money to buy (or refinance) the house plus the money to install the new windows and renovate the kitchen.

Often the loan will also include:

I.   An up to 20% "Contingency Reserved" so that you have the money to complete the project. In the event that the estimation of the cost end up being more than what was initially estimated.

II.   The loan may also include a provision that give you up to six months of mortgage payment so that you may live elsewhere while the repairs are being made.

There are two types of 203k loans. The first is the regular 203k, which is for properties that require structural repair such as room additions. The second is the streamline 203k which is given for non-structural repairs such as cosmetic work and appliances. FHA 203k loans don't cover "luxury improvements" such as installing Jacuzzis, or adding a pool. However FHA 203k loans will cover: flooring such as decks, patios and interior flooring, pluming, second stories, and bathrooms. Heating and Air Conditioning also qualify for FHA Financing.

▢   What is the max you can obtain for an FHA 203k loan?

Well it depends on which loan you apply for (Regular vs. Streamline)

1)   The as-is value of the property plus repairs.

Or

2)   110 Percent of the estimated value of the property once you do the repair (After- Value Repair).

*With a regular FHA 203k, the maximum amount you can get is the lesser of these two amounts.

In contrast with a 203k streamline loan. You can obtain the price of the home plus up to $35,000.

Note: To determine the as-is value of the property or the estimated value of the property after-repair value, you will need to have an appraisal done.

*An FHA loan requires you to put 3.5% down payment. However the down payment can come from a third party such as a family member.

What properties qualify for FHA Financing?

Properties that qualify are 1- to 4- family homes that has been completed for at least one year; a home that has been torn down but still has the foundation; a home that you can move to a new location. The home cannot be a co-op but a condo may qualify.

*You should always conduct a feasibility analysis with a qualified contractor whom will identify the repairs and upgrades required. You should also conduct a comparison of recently sold homes around the area to get an average price of the homes recently sold around the area. Remember that the FHA doesn't make loans, and that FHA doesn't sell homes.

Forum Clause- allows the parties to initiate litigation in a specific forum.

Forum Shopping- is the informal name given to the practice adopted by some litigants to have their legal case heard in the court that will likely rule in their favor.

Fair Debt Collection Practice Act- An act of congress which provides guidelines to collect debt, an entity may eliminate debt through this act by obtaining there credit report from www.annualcredit.com
        and dispute all negative debt 4 years or older by sending a validation letter the collection agency must furnish proof that you owe that money.

Fair Credit Billing Act- 15 U.S.C. §1601: allows you to dispute "billing errors" e.g. if you didn't receive the merchandise your entitled to a full refund.

Financial Structure- makeup of the right hand side of a company's Balance Sheet, which includes all the ways assets are finance. Such as trade accounts payable and short-term borrowings as well as long-term debt and ownership equity.

LETTER G

Grantor- The seller of a property i.e. real property (real estate)

Grantee- is the entity receiving title to a piece of property i.e. real property (real estate)

Greenlake Capital LLC v. Bingo Investments, LLC 185Cal.App.4th731(2010) Common law in California which allows a party to contract with another party to assist in seeking financing for its business operations.

LETTER H

Habituation- the tendency of a person to use adaptive behavior regularly that such behavior becomes unconscious.

Home equity- The difference between what the real property is worth i.e. the fair market value and what is owed on the property. In bankruptcy home equity is protected from creditors, other things protected from creditors are individual retirement accounts and motor vehicles. See Title 11 U.S.C. § 522(d)

Homestead- a document filed in the county recorder's office which protects some home equity from force sale of the property.

Heir- A person who, under the laws of intestacy, is entitled to receive an instate descendant's property, especially real property.

GLOSSARY I

IPR- An acronym for "Inter-parties review"

Inter-parties review- A procedure brought before the U.S. Patent and Trademark office. The department responsible to review IPR's is the Patent Trial and Appeal Boards (PTAB) which reviews the patentability of an issue based on certain novelty, obviousness (35 U.S.C. § 103) and anticipation(35 U.S.C. § 102)grounds.

*"Novelty" means: new. See link below for reference on novelty definition: https://www.law.cornell.edu/wex/novel

** "Obviousness" means: If a person skilled in the art can come up with your invention based on prior art then your invention is obvious. See link for reference on non-obviousness definition: https://www.law.cornell.edu/wex/nonobviousness

*** "Anticipation" means: that your patent is invalidated due to prior invention or prior disclosure of the invention. See link below for reference on anticipation: https://www.law.cornell.edu/wex/anticipation

Inequitable Doctrine: A defense to a patent infringement suit in which a defendant challenges the patentee's patent and alleges that the U.S. patent and trademark office would have not issue the patent. If the patentee would have disclosed certain misrepresented omitted information material to patentability and patentee fail to disclose the information with the specific intent to mislead or deceive the U.S. patent and trademark office. This defense requires complex pleading, due dillignece and discovery.

ITC- Acronym for International Trade Commission.

International Trade Commision- Can order an "exclusion order" on patent infringers. An the "exclusion order" authorizes the U.S. government to seize patent infringed products.

Installment Agreement- An agreement to purchase real property. Installment Agreement is treated as a wrap around mortgage. In this type of installment agreement the contract price is equal to the gross sales price.

Intentional wrong- A wrong in which "mens rea" (Guilty mind) amounts to intention, purpose, or design- Also termed willful wrong.

Incorporated by reference- A method of making a secondary document part of a primary document by including a statement that the secondary document should be treated as if it were contained within the primary one.

Intrigration Clause- A contractual provision stating that the contract represents the parties complete and final agreement ans supersedes all informal understandings and oral agreements relating to the subject matter of the contract also termed merger clause; entire contract clause.

Indeminifacation- The act of compensating a person for loss or a damage sustained.

Indemnification Clause- A clause in a contract that protects a person from loss or damage.

Intangible property- Property that doesn't exist physically e.g. Business good will or stock options.

Improvement patent-A patent that improves a pre-existing patent. Once a patent is improved both parties are required to obtain licenses from each other to practice each other patent's.

Investment Company Act of 1940- Regulates exchange traded funds, face-amount certificates, close-end funds, mutual funds (pools money to buy securities) and the investment industry.

Invoice- a list of goods sent or services provided, with a statement of the sum due for these services or goods.

Income statement (Profit and Loss Statement)- A financial statement which show the business revenues and where they are coming from and the expenses of the business.

"Investment adviser"- under the California Corporation Code Section 25009 means any person who, for compensation, engages in the business of advising others, either directly or through publications or writings, as to the value of securities or as to the advisability of investing in, purchasing or selling securities, or who, for compensation and as a part of a regular business, publishes analyses or reports concerning securities."

*Which would be a great person for you to use such "financial adviser" to sell your securities to "accredited investors" or other depending on your offering.

LETTER J

Joint Venture- "A joint venture is 'an undertaking by two or more persons jointly to carry out a single business enterprise for profit.' " (Weiner v. Fleischman(1991) 54 Cal.3d 476, 482 [286 Cal.Rptr. 40, 816 P.2d 892], internal citations omitted.) "A joint venture has been defined in various ways, but most frequently perhaps as an association of two or more persons who combine their property, skill or knowledge to carry out a single business enterprise for profit." (Holtz v. United Plumbing and Heating Co. (1957) 49 Cal.2d 501, 506 [319 P.2d 617].) Joint ventures are similar to partnerships, but the term "joint venture" commonly applies to temporary business arrangements involving a single transaction: "From a legal standpoint, both relationships are virtually the same. Accordingly, the courts freely apply partnership law to joint ventures when appropriate." (Weiner, supra, 54 Cal.3d at p. 482.) "It has generally been recognized that in order to create a joint venture there must be an agreement between the parties under which they have a community of interest, that is, a joint interest, in a common business ndertaking, an understanding as to the sharing of profits and losses, and a right of joint control." (Holtz, supra, 49 Cal.2d at pp. 506-507.) "The joint enterprise theory, while rarely invoked outside the automobile accident context, is well established and recognized in this state as an exception to the general rule that imputed liability for the negligence of another will not be recognized." (Christensen v. Superior Court(1991) 54 Cal.3d 868, 893 [2 Cal.Rptr.2d 79, 820 P.2d 181], internal citation omitted.)

"The existence or nonexistence of a joint venture is a fact question for resolution by the jury." (Kaljian v. Menezes (1995) 36 Cal.App.4th 573, 586 [42 Cal.Rptr.2d 510], internal citations omitted.)

Joint Stock Company- A form of business structure that combines the features of a corporation and a partnership under U.S. law, Joint stock companies are recognize as corporations.

Joint tenancy- Ownership of an asset by two or more persons, each of whom have an undivided interest with the right of survivorship meaning that if one dies the other can take over the property without probate.

Joint tortfeasors- Two or more individuals who either:

(1)   Act in concern to commit a tort. "Concern" is equivalent to criminal accessory or conspirator (aids or encourages another to commit a tort)

(2)   Act independently but cause a single indivisible tortiors injury, or

(3)   Share responsibility because of vicarious liability.

LETTER K

Keogh Plan- Also known as an HR-10 plan: which permit a self-employed individual to set aside certain percentage of compensation in a trust each year and to deduct this amount on tax return as an ordinary business expense, this money can be invested by the trust on behalf of the individual, and all earnings and gains on these investments are compounded tax-free. Tax are due when the Keogh plan is distributed.

LETTER L

Luxury of convenience- What a person is willing to pay for instant gratification.

Limited Liability Company- *(L.L.C.)- A company formed by filling articles of organization with the secretary of state. Usually an L.L.C. has an operating agreement that shows the relation between its members.

Left digit effect- A pricing strategy that makes a sum look affordable for example $9.95 the $10.00 is reduce to left by 5 cent making it the product appear more affordable.

Legal title- The person who is the owner of property or land.

Listing Agreement- An agreement between a seller, an a broker to list the property for sale in exchange for a commission once the property is sold. There is two types of listing agreements:

(1)   "Open listing agreement"- which means that if the seller brings in a buyer the broker gets no commission.

(2)   "Exclusive Listing Agreement"- means that there is only one broker that handles everything.

Legal Wrong- An Act that is a violation of the law; an act authoritatively prohibited by a rule of law.

LETTER M

Membership Interest- An interest in the decision's made by a limited liability company in other words the right to notice, vote in an L.L.C.

Mail Fraud- A Statue enacted by U.S. Congress in which (1) there is a scheme to defraud and (2) the mailing of matter is for the exclusive purpose of executing the scheme. See e.g. Pereida v. United States (1954) 347 U.S.; "Mail fraud" is namely, to prohibit misuse of mail to further a fraudulent enterprise. See e.g. U.S. v. Kelem 416 F.2d 346 (1970)).

Mortgage REIT- it's a mortgage real estate investment trust that lends money to builders and buyers.

Mens rea-[Law latin "guilty mind"] The state of mind that the prosecution, to secure the conviction, must prove that a defendant had when coming a crime; criminal intent or recklessness.

Mastermind principle- Napoleone Hill's principal in which you work with other harmoniously to achieve more than what you can do in a lifetime, in a year.

Mortgage loan originator- (California Law)- is someone who takes a residential mortgage loan application or offers or negotiates terms for residential mortgages.

*Individual who conduct loan processing or underwrite, must hold a real estate broker license with a MLO (Mortgage Loan Originator) License endorsement. See more information on the link below: http://www.dre.ca.gov/Licensees/MLOLicense.html#3

See also: http://www.dre.ca.gov/files/pdf/re19.pdf

For Other publications See: http://www.dre.ca.gov/Publications/CompleteListPublications.html

Master Limited Partnership- A publicly traded limited partnership.

LETTER N

NPE- Acronym for non-practicing entity.

Non-practcing entity- A person or company that goes around with their patents and they try to license their patents for money.

Neurobiology- The study of brain and the chemicals in it and the various function's of the brain.

Novation Clause- Is a clause in a contract that allows the substitution of a new party to a contract and the release of an existing party.

Negligence- The failure to exercise the standard of care that a reasonably prudent person would have exercise in similar situation; any conduct that falls below the legal standard established to protect other against unreasonable conduct that is intentionally, wantonly, or willing disregardful of others' rights.

LETTER O

Offer- In reference to contracts an indication that the person making an offer (the offeror)is seeking an exchange of some sort with another person (the offeree) and is willing to legally bound to the exchange if the offeree indicates a similar willingness to be bound by accepting the offer.

Offering- The act of presenting something to a person for acceptance.

LETTER P

Pooling and serving agreement- A documents which states the rights and obligations of a certain parties and how the trust is created and funded. This document is used in mortgage backed securities.

Proxy- One who is authorized to act as a substitute for another; especially in corporate law, a person who is authorize to vote another's stock shares. 2. The grant of authority by which a person is so authorized. 3. The document granting this authority.

Personal Holding Company- a holding company that is subject to special taxes and that usually has limited number of share holders, with most of its revenue originating from passive income such as dividends, interest, rent, and royalties.

Paralegal- A person who assist a lawyer in duties related to practice of law but who is not licensed attorney.- Also termed legal assistant, legal analyst.

Paralegalized- Slag to proofread, cite check and double-check the details in a legal document.

PTRC- Acronym for Patent and trademark resources center.

Procedural Knowledge- Is specific knowledge relating to performing tasks. Also in reference to intellectual property it means a "trade secret" See. Declarative Knowledge.

Passbook Loan- is a loan that is out of your own passbook savings account. Basically you go to a bank an open a passbook savings account and borrow your own money from the bank, the bank charges you interest *(low-interest) and it reports it to the credit bureaus. However you should verify that your bank reports your payment of the passbook loan. Once you make final payment and establish a positive track record then you could apply for an unsecure loan.

Piggyback credit- is a way of boosting up your credit score by two methods:

1.   Is becoming an "authorize user" on someone else's account it enables you to have his or her credit history reported on your credit.

2.   Second way of piggyback credit would be to obtain a cosigner, but this is usually not recommended because the cosigner's credit history doesn't show up on your credit report. Instead all that shows up is your own payment history and if you default, the default shows up on the cosigners' credit history and it stays there for seven years (NOT RECOMMENDED).

Preapproved (Real Estate Loans) - Is simply an estimate of how much the lender is willing to lend you. Provide how much you make and how much you plan to put as a down payment. Then the lender will provide you with an estimate on the amount of your mortgage payment you will potentially be paying. However there is no commitment involved by either party.

Prequalified (Real Estate Loans) – is similar to preapproved however there is usually a fee involved because your credit is run and the lender commits to lending you the money.

Public-exchange Offer- An attempt to take over a corporation by offering to exchange some of its securities for a specified number of targeted corporations voting shares.

Private offering- An offering made only to a small number of accredited investor's or, an offering made to a small group of interested buyers.

Promoter- Someone who starts or organizes a corporation or business venture.

Partnership- An association of two or more persons who jointly own and carry on a business entity for profit. A partnership is presumed existing under the uniform partnership act if the person's agree to share the business's profits or losses.

For more information on the uniform partnership act visit this link: http://www.uniformlaws.org/shared/docs/partnership/upa_final_97.pdf

Pioneer Patent- A patent covering a function major advance that has never been performed, a completely new device, or patentable subject matter that is new and important that it progresses the art and is distinguish from a mere improvement or perfection of what had gone before.

LETTER Q

QM- Acronym for qualified mortgage

Qualified Mortgage- A mortgage that a person may qualify for if there Debt-to-Income ration is less than 43% For more information on qualified mortgage visit: http://files.consumerfinance.gov/f/201312_cfpb_mortgagerules.pdf

Quorum- The number of people "members" or "Stock holders" for a meeting to be valid in a corporation or society.

LETTER R

Regulation A- Is a direct public offering. See Chapter 2 for an actual description.

Regulation S- a "safe harbor" regulation under the securities Act of 1933 which exempt an offering from registration so long as the offering is done offshore further resells of the stock must be made offshore i.e. outside of the United States.

Real Estate Settlement Procedure Act (RESPA)- Prevents the use of undisclosed kickbacks and prevent unlicensed professionals from obtaining money from real estate transactions.

Restatement- is an influential treatise on tort law issued by the American Law Institute.

Right of First Refusal- A contractual right of an "entity" to be given the opportunity to enter into a business transaction with a person before anyone else can. Since an "entity" has a right, but not an obligation, to enter into a transaction that generally involves an asset. If the entity with the right of first refusal declines to enter into a transaction the owner is free to open the bidding up to other interested parties.

Right of rescission- A right in a contract to cancel it within a certain period of time, The right of rescission can be added to any contract. For more information on rescission clause on mortgages click this link: http://www.bankrate.com/finance/mortgages/law-gives-3-days-to-cancel-refi-or-heloc-1.aspx

LETTER S

Structure- A pattern of organization such as schematics in electronics leading a desire result.

Settlement- The several definitions are described below:

1.   Estate (Settlement): Distribution of an estate's assets by an executor to beneficiaries after all legal procedures have been completed.

2.   Law (Settlement): Agreement reached through negotiation.

3.   Real Estate (Settlement): date when the real property is purchased (or sold) and the deed is transferred to the buyer.

 Shared-appreciation mortgage (SAM)- Residential loan with a fixed interest rate set below market rates. In which the lender is entitled to a specific share of appreciation in property value over a specific time interval.

Secondary Considerations (Patent Law)- Are used to overcome "obviousness. These Secondary considerations are:

1.   Long-felt need

2.   Failure of others

3.   Commercial success

4.   Commercial acquiescence via licensing

5.   Professional Approval

6.   Copying and praise from infringers

7. Progress through PTO (patent Trademark Office)

8. Near simultaneous invention

9. Unexpected results

Settlor- A person who settles property on trust law for the benefit of beneficiaries. In some legal systems, a settler is usually referred to as a trustor, granto or donor. In testimary trust the settler is usually referred to as the testator.

Shared-equity mortgage (SEM)- Home loan in which the lender is granted a share of the equity, threby allowing the lender to participate in the proceeds from resale.

Shareholders equity- Total assets minus liabilities of a corporation, also known as stockholders equity and net worth.

Shell Corporation-

1. A company that is incorporated but has no significant assets or operations. Such a corporation may be formed to obtain financing prior to starting operations.

2. Corporation set up by fraudulent operations as a front to conceal tax evasion schemes.

Surety- The person who has pledge him or herself to payback money or perform a certainaction if the principal to a contract fails.

Seller Concession- "Seller contributions" What the seller contributions at closing for the benefit of the buyer.

Security Act of 1933- The federal law regulating the registration and initial public offering of securities. Also termed the securities act.

See also:

Securities Act of 1933- A U.S. federal statute codified in Title 15 U.S.C. § 77 et.seq. enacted after the stock market crash of 1929 requiring that companies to register their securities prior to offering them to investors in primary markets.

Securities Exchange Act of 1934- The federal law regulating the public trading of securities. This law provides for the registration and supervision of securities exchanges and brokers and proxy solicitations. The act establishes the SEC "Securities and Exchange Act" See 15 U.S.C. § 78a et seq. – Also termed Exchange Act; 1934 Act.

Smith Act of 1948- A federal anti-sedition law that criminalizes advocating the forcible or violent overthrow of government 18 U.S.C. § 2385

Small Business Investment Company- A corporation created under state law to provide long-term equity capital to small businesses, as provided under the Small business administration 15 U.S.C. § 661 et seq.- Abbr. SBIC. See link for more info on SBIC: https://www.sba.gov/content/sbic-directory for more information on funding stages see this link: http://www.entrepreneur.com/article/42336

Statue at large- An official compilation of acts and resolutions that become law from sessions of congress, printed in chronological order.

Stop and frisk- A police officers brief detention, questioning, and search of a person for a conceal weapon when the officer reasonably suspects that the person has committed a crime. The stop and frisk, which can be conducted without a warrant or probable cause was held constitutional by the supreme court in Terry v. Ohio, 392 U.S. 1, 88 S. Ct. 1868 (1968) Also termed investigatory stop; Terry stop.

Secure Credit Card- It's a credit card that can be obtained after you establish a savings account and build up the balance. Once you build up the balance you could pledge your saving account balance against your secure credit card and then after successful payments on your secure credit card. Then the bank will allow you to get a regular credit card. The payments on the secure credit card are usually reported to the three major credit bureaus and can help you build a history and a credit score.

Surviving Partner- A partner who serves as a trustee of the partnership once one of the partners dies and the surviving partner is responsible for administering the partnership remaining affairs.

Subrogation- The substitution of one party for another in which the party that is substituted is relief and the other party pays the debt of the party relief and is therefore entitled to the rights, remedies, and securities of the original debtor who was substituted.

LETTER S

Shelf Corporation- A corporation that was established that has no current operations. A shelf corporation is perfect to attain investors and/or credit. However if the credit bureau find out that the corporation has new management they will rated as "re-aging" which can reduce your ability to attain credit or investors. A shelf corporation is also known as a shell corporation

LETTER T

Trustee-An entity with the vested power to administer the property in a trust for the benefit of a beneficiary.

The Service member Civil relief Act- A law that protects military personnel from eviction, auto lease cancellation penalties, high interest rates, and being summoned to a court learning while serving.

Telephone Consumer Protection Act- A law designated to restrict unsolicited calls by telemarketers. Such calls are limited to the hours of 8 a.m. to 9 p.m. and there is the do not call list See Additional resources to obtain the number to get on the do not call list.

Tangible property- Property that has form and can be touched.

Transferable interest- A right in a limited liability company to obtain distributions from the profits made from profitable operations.

Truth in Lending Act of 1987- An act to safeguard the consumer in connection with the utilization of credit by requiring full disclosure of terms and conditions of finance charged in credit transaction.

Trust- Is a fiduciary agreement that allows a 3rd party, or trustee, to hold assets on behalf of a beneficiary or beneficiaries (Usually avoids probate court).

Tortfeasor- One who commits a tort, a wrongdoer.

Trust Company- A company that acts as a trustee for people and entities and that sometimes also operates as a commercial bank.

The credit card accountability, responsibility and disclosure act (CARD Act): Protects you from unfair credit card billing practices. It's designed e.g. to prevent overcharging for late fee's on credit cards.

LETTER V

Vacarious liability- is a form of tort liability that holds a "respondeat superior" liable for hisfailure to stop what caused the injury.

LETTER W

Writ of Administrative mandamus- "Generally, a Petition for Writ of Administrative Mandamus is a request that a Superior Court review and reverse the final decision or order of an administrative agency".

http://sandiegolawlibrary.org/wpcontent/uploads/2013/04/Writ_of_Administrative_Mandamus.pdf

Writ of mandate- A writ of mandate is a document filed with a court to compel a government body, official, corporation, or individual to perform a duty it is required to perform, or allow a lawful right to be exercised. See California Code of Civil Procedure § 1085

*If you are a felon familiarize yourself with this business and professional code §§ 480-489 et seq. This is the link to that business and professional code: http://www.leginfo.ca.gov/cgi-bin/displaycode?section=bpc&group=00001-01000&file=480-489

Also check this California Supreme Court Case: "Newland v. Board of Governors (1977) 19 Cal.3d 705, 711" See the case at the link below:

http://scocal.stanford.edu/opinion/newland-v-board-governors-30444

***Computer Terms Reference Guide:

http://cdn.ttgtmedia.com/CascadingTargetedDownloads/downloads/TechTarget%20IT%20Acronyms.pdf

Wraparound mortgage- is a "private mortgage" in which the buyer makes payments directly to the seller and the indebtness of the property. This type of "private mortgage" leaves the mortgage liability on the seller. The buyer doesn't assume the mortgage therefore avoiding capital gain taxes. The wrap around mortgage includes the unpaid balance of the underlying indebtness, in the form of installment payments. The wrap around mortgage is a good method to avoid (transfer taxes) Capital gain taxes on property with an excess of basis. The seller who finances real property with a wraparound mortgage must report an installment sale on IRS form 6252 and should report the installment sale income on Schedule D or on IRS form 4797for your taxable gain. It is said that a wrap-around mortgage is not assume but deemed cancel, meaning that the "Due on sale clause" cannot be enforced.

Writ of Coram Nobis- See Coram Nobis

Writ of sequestration- A writ ordering that a court be given custody of something, or order that something not bhe taken from the jurisdiction, such as collateral for a promissory note.

Writ of restitution- The process of enforcing a civil judgement in a forcible-entry and detainer motion or enforcing restitution on a verdict in a criminal protection for forcible entry and detainer.

www.ingramcontent.com/pod-product-compliance
Lightning Source LLC
Chambersburg PA
CBHW080624180526

45168CB00007B/3047